# AI Mastery Unleashed

## The Ultimate ChatGPT Resource Vault

Dive into 40,000+ Prompts, 193 Expert Videos and a World of Digital Innovation – Your All-In-One Guide to Navigating the AI Frontier for Businesses, Students, Professionals and all Curious Minds Alike!

"In a time not distant, it will be possible to flash any image formed in thought on a screen and render it visible at any place desired. The perfection of this means of reading thought will create a revolution for the better in all our social relations."

Nikola Tesla

Published by Lorean Publishing House

First Edition: November 2023

# Disclaimer

This book is for informational purposes only. The author and publisher have tried to be accurate, but there might be errors. The prompts and examples in this book are just that - examples. They aren't guarantees. The author and publisher aren't responsible for how you use this information or any results from it. Use it at your own risk.

Any mentioned third-party tools or services are for reference only and are not endorsed or guaranteed by the author or publisher.

# A Note from the Author

Dear Valued Explorer,

Welcome to a journey where technology and creativity intersect, leading us towards a future pulsating with endless possibilities.

The inception of "AI Mastery Unleashed: The Ultimate ChatGPT Resource Vault" was birthed from a simple spark - a curiosity that led to venturing into the enthralling world of ChatGPT and Artificial Intelligence. What unfurled was an odyssey of exploration and discovery, revealing a cosmos where digital wizardry and human ingenuity collide, unlocking realms that were once only imaginable in our dreams.

Today, this eBook stands not merely as a repository but as a concise compilation designed to empower, enlighten and guide you through the almost limitless possibilities of AI and ChatGPT to assist you in achieving your goals.

 This is not just a guide. It's a galaxy of over 40,000 tools, prompts and courses, bound together to fuel your endeavours, whether they lie in the realms of business, personal projects or educational pursuits. It's a key to a universe where your innovative ideas blend with avant-garde technology, enabling you to shape your path to achieving your most aspiring dreams.

Your journey isn't just an adventure through the digital cosmos but also a step towards sculpting your own place in the vast landscapes of technology and AI. It's a treasure trove of resources that will act as a catalyst, propelling you into greater heights where your creativity and technological advancements fuse, enabling you to craft narratives that fast track you to success.

Let's start this journey together and delve deep into AI, traversing through the vast terrains of ChatGPT. It will allow you to intertwine exploration, knowledge and collaborative spirit where technology and human creativity coalesce into a wonderful blend of infinite possibilities.

I extend to you, my sincerest gratitude, for choosing to embark on this exciting expedition into the universes of ChatGPT and AI with this invaluable guide. Your engagement is a bold step into a community that thrives on shared wisdom, explorative minds and a boundless hunger for knowledge.

Here's to the future we forge, the adventures we embark upon and the many stories we will write in the digital expanse.

Warmly,

Dr. Alex Veridian

**"AI Mastery Unleashed: The Ultimate ChatGPT Resource Vault."**

Step into the Future with Over 40,000 + AI Tools, Prompts and Exclusive Courses - A Limitless Universe for Businesses, Personal Projects, Education, Professional and all Curious Minds Alike!

**Navigate the Infinite:** Unveil the Ultimate ChatGPT Mastery Bundle! A bountiful harvest of over 29,000 ChatGPT Prompts, including a Mega Bonus, tailor-made to empower every sector of your digital world - be it personal, business or educational!

**Envision an All-Encompassing Hub of Knowledge and Tools,** with a myriad of applications across various domains of ChatGPT, AI and digital marketing. Indulge in 33 video sessions of 'Prompt Engineering Mastery', unearth wisdom from 'The Art of Prompt Engineering' eBook, explore the nuances with the 'ChatGPT-4 Guide' and unlock a universe designed meticulously for individuals, professionals, businesses and students!

**Discover a trove** that's more than just a collection - it's your passport to uncharted territories in the AI and digital landscape. Whether you are an entrepreneur sculpting your digital presence, a student exploring futuristic tech, or an individual enriching personal projects, this bundle is a vessel designed to transport you through the endless oceans of AI possibilities and digital marvels!

Elevate Your Journey with this unparalleled bundle today and redefine how you interact with the digital world. You will not only unlock a wealth of knowledge and tools but also become an integral part of a movement that blends innovation, shared wisdom and tangible contributions towards a powerhouse of knowledge.

# Table of Contents

b. <u>ChatGPT Mastery Course 62 Videos</u>

Dive Deep into Prompt Engineering

c. <u>Prompt Engineering eBook"The Art of Prompt Engineering with ChatGPT"</u>

Chat

d. <u>GPT Search Planner</u>

Multiverse of Tools

e. <u>ChatGPT- 4 Guide and 1,500 + AI Tools</u>

f. 2,500 + Digital Product Ideas - Mega Bonus

Prompts Galore

g. <u>12,000+ ChatGPT Prompts</u>

h.    <u>29,000+ Bonus Bundle of Prompts</u>

Exclusive Courses

SaaS ChatGPT Course

i.    <u>33 Videos + 500 Prompts</u>

ChatGPT Power Course

j.    <u>25 + Videos</u>

Email and Marketing

k.    <u>325 Email Marketing ChatGPT Prompts</u>

l.   <u>50 WordPress ChatGPT Prompts</u>

## Cheat Sheets and Guides

m.   <u>The Ultimate Canva Cheatsheet</u>

n.   <u>Notion Creator's ChatGPT Cheat Sheet</u>

## Productivity and Automation

o.   <u>365+ Automation Templates</u>

p.   <u>500+ Productivity Resources</u>

# Additional Resources

### q. Full ChatGPT Prompts + Resources

### r. 500+ Best ChatGPT Prompts

# Search and Planning

### s. ChatGPT Search Planner

### t. 2,000 + ChatGPT Prompts

# PowerPoint Presentation

### u. Presentation & Free Gift

"I'm optimistic about the potential of AI to make the world a better place. But it's important to be careful and responsible about how we develop and use it. We need to make sure that AI is aligned with human values and that it benefits all of humanity."

Mark Zuckerberg

**Embarking on a Digital Odyssey with ChatGPT:**

Dive into the heart of ChatGPT, where each question or request isn't just a tool but a shining guide, helping you explore the vast world of AI conversations.

These 4,000 ChatGPT prompts are like your co-pilots, skilfully navigating the complexities of language, helping you create interesting and meaningful digital conversations that reach people clearly and profoundly across the internet.

**A Cosmos of Possibilities with ChatGPT Prompts:**

Each expert ChatGPT prompt holds countless possibilities, where the magic of technology and human creativity combine to create digital conversations that go beyond just talking.

As you explore these carefully selected prompts, you'll not only see the huge scope of what AI can do but also find places where your own creative ideas work hand in hand with ChatGPT's abilities. This helps shape a future where your online conversations are as imaginative as the universe itself.

**Practical Manifestations Across Multiple Sectors:**

Imagine these ChatGPT prompts as valuable tools in real life situations covering a multitude of  fields like online shopping, education, content creation, customer support and much more! They greatly enhance these sectors by providing smart, relevant and interesting conversations for every interaction, like bright stars illuminating the way.

- **E-Commerce Constellations:** Imagine virtual shopping assistants, powered by ChatGPT prompts, that guide users through a personalised and captivating shopping experience, intertwining product knowledge with conversational charm.

- **Educational Nebulas:** Envision digital tutors, equipped with our clever prompts, fostering a nurturing and engaging learning environment, where every question is met with insightful and empathetic responses, sculpting a supportive and exciting educational journey.

- **Content Creation Galaxies:** Picture your content creation journey where ChatGPT prompts infuse your narratives with pulsating life, ensuring each word resonates with authentic and compelling vibrancy, engaging your audience and guiding them through your created universes.

- **Customer Support Meteors:** Picture customer support bots, empowered by these prompts, seamlessly navigating through the vastness of customer queries, ensuring every interaction is a journey of support, understanding and resolution.

**Engineering Dialogues that Echo in the Digital Eternity:**

As you make use of these 4,000 ChatGPT prompts, think of each one as a building block for creating conversations that make a lasting impact in the digital world. They help ensure that every word, message and interaction isn't just sent but makes a lasting impression with your online audience.

**Explore 4,000+ ChatGPT Prompts Here**

# Embarking on a Creative Odyssey with the MEGA BONUS: 2,500 Digital Product Ideas!

## Unleashing the Creative Nebula:

Get ready to explore our exciting MEGA BONUS, where 2,500 Digital Product Ideas aren't just random suggestions; they come together like a bright and creative nebula. They're here to add innovation to your projects. Think of this bonus as a door to a universe filled with creative energy. Each idea is like a spark that can start something big in your online creative world. These ideas are more than just suggestions; they're like seeds waiting to grow into amazing innovations. They'll make sure your journey is not only full of creativity but they'll also keep you inspired along the way.

**A Spectrum of Inventive Potentials:**

With the MEGA BONUS, you'll discover a wide range of digital product ideas. Each of them has the potential to adapt and fit into your own creative vision, whatever your speciality. These ideas cover various arenas, from e-books, apps and online courses to software, interactive platforms and so much more.

Think of each idea like a unique entity in space, ready to combine and adapt to your vision. They'll help you craft products and services that aren't just innovative but also reflect your own distinct creative touch, making them stand out in the digital world.

**Crafting Your Digital Projects:**

1. **Guiding Your Way:** Think of these 2,500 ideas as your compass to help you navigate through the vast possibilities. They'll make sure every product or service you create is both cutting edge and useful.

2. **Customising Outstanding Products:** Embark on a journey where each idea can be customised, shaped and adjusted to match your own ideas and the ever-changing digital landscape. This ensures that everything you create reflects your own innovation and meets the ever-evolving requirements of the online world.

3. **Crafting Memorable Stories:** Make sure that each project tells a story, like a narrative that travels through the digital universe. It should connect with and engage every person it comes across in the online universe, leaving a lasting impression.

**Creating Practical and Lasting Impact:**

1.  **Digital Blacksmithing:** Blend the practical strength of real-world usefulness with the imaginative essence of creativity. This means that each idea isn't just created but forged in a special mix of inventive and practical magic.

2.  **Navigating Cosmic Challenges:** Use these ideas as a guide through the complex challenges of digital creation. This ensures that every product not only solves problems but also gracefully moves through the maze of user needs and digital requirements.

3.  **Crafting Magical Experiences:** Make sure that every digital product you create doesn't just serve a purpose but captivates its users, creating experiences that linger in their memories long after they've used it.

**Becoming a Digital Universe Architect:**

Your exploration of these 2,500 digital product ideas isn't just about discovery: it's about being a creative architect. Each idea is like a building block, helping you construct a universe where every digital product is like a star, gracefully revolving around the needs, wishes and dreams of its users.

Let each idea be a journey where creativity and practicality come together in harmony, making sure that everything you create isn't just used, but truly appreciated and treasured in the vast digital world.

Unlock Your
MEGA BONUS Here

"Artificial intelligence is the most important
technological development in human history."
Jeff Bezos

# Mastering Google Drive Downloads: A Step-by-Step Guide

**Navigating Through the Digital Realm**

As we delve into the dynamic space of Google Drive, this guide is dedicated to amplifying your mastery over managing, organising and utilising downloaded resources in the digital cloud. The intricate paths of storing and maintaining digital resources become pivotal, especially when every file is a cornerstone for your projects and endeavours.

1. **Introduction to the Digital Storage Phenomenon:**

   - **Understanding Downloads:** Take a glimpse into the core of downloading files, exploring its nuances and understanding its pertinence in preserving essential digital artefacts.

- **The Essence of Storing:** Beyond just saving your work, there is a paradigm where each file, when stored efficiently, becomes a potent tool readily available at your fingertips.

2. **Structuring and Managing Your Digital Space:**

   - **Organising Files:** An in-depth exploration into categorising and structuring your files to create a streamlined and navigable storage environment.

   - **Optimised Use:** Techniques that ensure that every megabyte of your cloud space is utilised to its full potential, fostering an environment of growth, sustainability and manageability.

3. **The Art and Science of Efficient File Management:**

   - **Innovative Storage Solutions:** A guide through crafting storage strategies that ensure longevity and easy accessibility of data.

   - **Redefining Resource Management:** Unlock methodologies that redefine conventional file management, turning each download into a pivotal resource for your digital pursuits.

4. **Seamless Accessibility and Sharing:**

   - **Strategic Access Management:** Understand and implement strategic access management, ensuring the right files are accessible when and where they're needed.

   - **Collaborative Ecosystem:** Creating and managing a collaborative digital space, where sharing becomes effortless and collaborative efforts are maximised.

5. **Secure and Preserve Your Digital Assets:**

- **Safety Protocols:** Establish and implement strategies to safeguard your data, ensuring its integrity and availability when needed.

- **Digital Preservation:** Techniques and strategies aimed at ensuring the longevity and persistent availability of your digital resources.

6. **Tailoring Google Drive to Your Endeavours:**

- **Customisation Techniques:** A walkthrough of personalising Google Drive to resonate with your work patterns and project requirements.

- **Automating Processes:** Leverage automation within Google Drive to enhance efficiency and ensure a seamless operational flow.

**Closing Summary:**

Mastering Google Drive Downloads will transform your digital files into the valuable assets they are, streamlining your work and optimising your precious time. Organising downloads enhances efficiency and boosts project impact. This guide covers both technical aspects and will create an efficient, collaborative and secure digital workspace. Use it as a reliable companion for all your digital endeavours.

Special Feature:

Free Gift:

Dive into a realm of enhanced efficiency and infinite productivity with your free gift - "Productivity and Time Management for the Overwhelmed" complemented with a Bonus Video to elevate your journey.

Download the PowerPoint Presentation Here

# Unlocking Endless Possibilities with ChatGPT
## Navigate the Uncharted: An Exclusive Glimpse into Your Future with AI
### Embarking on a Journey of Digital Possibilities

This section methodically uncovers the plethora of possibilities unfurled by ChatGPT, an artificial intelligence model designed to navigate through the nuances of human language, offering a broad spectrum of applications that transcend conventional boundaries.

1. **Understanding ChatGPT:**

   - **Definition and Mechanics:**

     Navigate through the intricate machinery underpinning ChatGPT, understanding its architectural and operational framework.

   - **Underlying Principles:**

     Grasp the essential principles that drive ChatGPT's functionalities, shedding light on its language processing and generation capabilities.

2. **Wide-Ranging Applications of ChatGPT:**

   - **Business Optimization:**

     Explore how ChatGPT can streamline operations, enhance customer service, and fortify communication strategies within the business sphere.

   - **Educational Innovations:**

     Understand ChatGPT's role in augmenting educational experiences through personalised learning, automated assessment and interactive educational content.

   - **Creative Exploration:**

     Dive into how ChatGPT can be leveraged to enhance creative writing, ideation, and content generation, acting as a muse for creators across multiple disciplines.

3. **ChatGPT in Action: Real-World Impacts:**

- **Success Stories:**

  Traverse through a curated collection of real-world instances where ChatGPT has significantly impacted various industries and individual endeavours.

- **Challenges and Solutions:**

  Gain insights into the hurdles encountered in implementing ChatGPT and how innovative solutions have navigated through them.

4. **Future Focused: The Evolving Face of ChatGPT:**

- **Developments on the Horizon:**

  Envision the future trajectory of ChatGPT, exploring upcoming features, enhancements and potential expansions.

- **Integrating Emerging Technologies:**

  Understand how ChatGPT can intertwine with other emerging technologies, crafting a future where synergized tech creates unparalleled opportunities.

5. **Practical Integration of ChatGPT:**

- **Strategic Implementation:**

  Explore frameworks and strategies that facilitate the seamless integration of ChatGPT into various projects and operations.

- **Maximising Utility:**

  Grasp practical tips and best practices to harness the full potential of ChatGPT in a wide range of applications.

6. **Ethics and Responsible Use:**

- **Navigating Ethical Use:**

  Learn the importance and methodologies of employing ChatGPT ethically and responsibly in various scenarios.

- **Ensuring Equitable Access:**

  Understand the imperatives of ensuring broad and equitable access to technology and the strategies to facilitate it.

7. **Beyond the Horizon: Your Journey with ChatGPT:**

- **Participation in Advancement:**

  Grasp how your engagement with ChatGPT contributes to its evolution and the proliferation of AI technologies.

- **Continuous Exploration:**

  Be privy to a world where continuous exploration with ChatGPT leads to ongoing discoveries, innovative solutions and perpetually expanding possibilities.

**Concluding Reflections:**

In this meticulously curated section, the intention is to illuminate the boundless potentials and practical applications of ChatGPT in a multifaceted digital ecosystem. As we traverse through each subsection, you will find, not only valuable insights, but also ignite a spark that propels your projects and endeavours into new dimensions of innovation and success.

The ChatGPT Mastery Course, with its rich array of 62 in-depth videos, stands as a beacon of knowledge and expertise in the sprawling landscape of AI. Navigate through modules that unravel secrets of crafting effective prompts, deploying ChatGPT in various scenarios, and unlocking strategies that seamlessly blend technology with your everyday digital interactions.

Uncover strategies that not only enhance your communication with digital AI, but also sculpt it to be an intuitive extension of your digital self. Anticipate revelations on optimising prompt engineering, mastering user engagement and creating responsive AI interactions that resonate with your specific needs.

## Embark on the Mastery Journey Here

Embark on a literary and technical exploration with the eBook - "The Art of Prompt Engineering with ChatGPT". A wealth of insights, techniques and an amalgamation of art and technology, this eBook transcends being a normal guide, it's a trusted and helpful companion at your side as you weave through the various facets of utilising ChatGPT to its utmost potential.

## Highlighted Sneak Peek:

Imagine delving into pages that not only unravel the science behind the most effective prompts but also weave in the artistry required to make them truly impactful. The eBook carefully stitches together theoretical knowledge, practical strategies and a subtle undertone of crafting prompts that resonate, engage and perform.

### Explore the Art and Science Here

## Concluding Thoughts: A Horizon Unveiled

Where Insight Meets Action: Your Next Steps in the AI Adventure

As this section draws to a close, reflect upon the glimpses and sneak peeks into a future where your digital interactions are enriched, empowered and elegantly crafted through the capabilities of ChatGPT and the myriad of resources at your fingertips.

The snippets revealed in this section are but a mere drop in the ocean of knowledge, tools and potential encapsulated within this bundle. Each resource, tool and course stands ready to be unboxed by your curiosity, explored by your intellect and implemented in your digital adventures.

You're not merely a passenger on this journey; you are the navigator, crafting, moulding and steering your path through the boundless possibilities of AI and ChatGPT. Every click, every exploration from here on, is a step towards mastery, innovation and perhaps, the next big digital marvel.

As you step forth, remember: The future isn't written; it's crafted and with the tools, resources and knowledge contained herein, you hold the quill.

**Q1:** What makes this ChatGPT Mastery Bundle unique?

**A1:** The ChatGPT Mastery Bundle curates over 40,000 AI prompts, tools and exclusive video courses, providing unparalleled value for individuals and professionals across multiple sectors, ensuring there's something beneficial for everyone!

**Q2:** How can I access the ChatGPT Prompts and Tools?

**A2:** All the materials, including prompts and tools, can be reached by scanning the QR codes provided within the book, guiding you smoothly to the relevant content.

**Q3:** Are there any prerequisites for using these ChatGPT prompts and tools?

**A3:** No prerequisites are required. Both beginners and advanced users will find the resources helpful, with content ranging from basic to advanced levels.

**Q4:** Can I use these resources for my business/educational/personal projects?

**A4:** Absolutely! The bundle is crafted to be versatile, catering to business professionals, students, educators and individuals alike, enhancing any digital project you embark on.

**Q5:** Is there a time limit for accessing the resources once purchased?

**A5:** No, once you purchase the eBook, the resources contained within are yours to access indefinitely.

**Q6:** How can I access the 62-video ChatGPT Mastery Course?

**A6:** The Mastery Course can be accessed by scanning the QR codes which will direct you to the complete video series.

**Q7:** What if a QR Code is not working?

**A7:** While all QR Codes are meticulously checked, should you encounter any issues, please contact our support team at the end of this book for prompt assistance and resolution.

**Q8:** Can I share these resources with my team or colleagues?

**A8:** Yes, absolutely!

**Q9:** What type of content is covered in the 'Prompt Engineering Mastery' Video Course?

**A9:** The course delves into the intricacies of prompt engineering with ChatGPT, providing actionable insights, strategies and detailed walkthroughs across its 33 videos.

Q10: Is this Book beginner-friendly?

A10: Absolutely! The resources cater to all levels, ensuring beginners can navigate and utilise the content effectively while also providing immense value to advanced users.

Q11: Will there be updates to the Book or its resources?

A11: To ensure the optimal relevance and value, updates will be periodically made, and buyers will be notified accordingly to access the latest content.

Q12: Is there customer support available for queries or issues?

A12: Yes, our dedicated support team is available to assist you with any queries or issues you may encounter. Details at the end of this book.

Q13: What is the MEGA BONUS and how can it benefit me?

A13: The MEGA BONUS offers an additional 2,500 Digital Product Ideas, serving as a potent brainstorming tool for your digital projects, content creation and more.

Q14: Can I access the resources offline?

A14: While the Book can be accessed offline, the resources, being web-based (videos, tools, and additional prompts), will require an internet connection.

Q15: How does the PowerPoint presentation assist me in utilising Google Drive?

A15: The presentation provides a step-by-step guide on downloading and managing resources within Google Drive, ensuring smooth and efficient use.

Q16: Can I provide feedback on the Book and its resources?

A16: Certainly! We welcome and value your feedback, continually seeking to enhance the value and user experience of our offerings.

Q17: Are the resources compatible with all devices?

A17: The resources are crafted to be compatible across various devices, ensuring accessible and efficient use whether you're on a PC, tablet or mobile.

Q18: How can the ChatGPT Search Planner assist me?

A18: The ChatGPT Search Planner is designed to streamline your prompt utilisation, helping you strategically deploy and manage prompts for optimal results.

Q19: Are there any hidden fees or additional purchases required?

A19: No, the Book encompasses all mentioned resources without any hidden costs or subsequent purchases necessary.

Q20: How do I navigate the book effectively?

A20: Utilizing a detailed Table of Contents and QR codes that link to additional resources, finding the sections you need is both straightforward and convenient.

## Join Me on This Unparalleled Journey
## into the Expanses of ChatGPT and AI!

Thank you so much for choosing to dive deep into this comprehensive and resource-rich guide. Your pursuit of knowledge and innovation has led you here and it's genuinely exhilarating to share this vast digital opportunity with you.

While the abundance of information within these pages is extensive and teeming with possibilities, I invite you to navigate this journey with gentle curiosity and mindful exploration. Although the lure to immerse fully into every niche and subject may be tempting, consider first pinpointing a particular area that sparks your fascination or aligns with your immediate interests or needs.

**Tip for Your Exploration:**

Choose a favourite niche or subject and begin your exploration there. Allow yourself to traverse through the materials, insights and tools at a pace that feels enjoyable and digestible. This methodical approach ensures your exploration is fruitful, engaging and devoid of feeling overwhelmed. As you gradually unravel the layers and assimilate the knowledge, you'll discover that mastery and expertise are crafted in step-by-step, joyous learning.

Your presence, engagement and exploration within these digital realms are not just a leap towards sculpting your own future but are also an invaluable part of our collective journey towards an intertwining of astute human ingenuity and the boundless possibilities as technology unfolds.

Together, through every page you turn and each link you explore, we carve out our paths into a future that harmoniously weaves technology and humanity into a canvas of infinite possibilities.

With immense appreciation and excitement for the explorations ahead,


**Dr. Alex Veridian**

# Your Purchase is a Pivotal Step Towards a Thriving Digital Ecosystem

Your journey into this bundle isn't just a purchase that you use. It signifies a meaningful stride towards a more enriched, accessible and innovative digital landscape. The investment you've made in acquiring this vast repository of knowledge and tools is reciprocated with our unyielding commitment to continuously foster a digital environment where ideas flourish, solutions emerge and possibilities are endless through our creativity and imagination.

In traversing through the intricate realms of ChatGPT and AI together, we can embrace an era where technology, innovation and communal growth coalesce into a potent force for progression and transformation. Your engagement does not only fortify your own digital endeavours but also contributes to a broader ecosystem where advancements and innovations are ceaselessly propelled forward.

Journey further, explore deeper and stay curious and inspired! Let's continue to weave through the boundless territories of digital opportunities together, crafting a future where our collective pursuits in the technological dominions are perpetually ascending, exploring and innovating.

## Stay Connected and Continue the Exploration

The digital landscapes are ever evolving, and so are we. Your journey through the realms of AI and ChatGPT does not conclude here. In fact, consider this a launchpad into future adventures that promise more insights, resources, and discoveries in the fascinating world of artificial intelligence.

We invite you to remain intertwined with our explorations and be the first to access upcoming resources, offers, and exploratory ventures into the digital unknown. Your continuous engagement propels us forward, and your feedback crafts our trajectory.

"Essential AI Resource Vault"

1. The AI Income Database

A comprehensive databank to augment your AI knowledge and applications.

2. Transforming Photos into Cartoons with Midjourney

Discover the art of digital photo transformation.

3.  FutureTools

An organised collection of cutting-edge AI tools to enhance your digital prowess.

4.  Best Midjourney Prompts

Dive into 644 innovative text-to-image ideas that promise to spark creativity.

5.  V4 Midjourney Reference Sheets

A consolidated guide to enhance your Mid Journey explorations.

6.  Midjourney Prompt Helper

An assistive tool tailored for optimising prompt crafting and utilisation.

7. ChatGPT Advanced Data Analysis Prompts

Elevate your data analytics with these specially curated prompts.

8. PromptStorm - ChatGPT, Bard, Claude Prompts

A browser integration to simplify and enhance your prompt-based interactions across ChatGPT, Bard, and Claude.

9. Midjourney Cheat Sheet

A concise guide for quick referencing and efficient Midjourney navigation.

10. The Prompt Report Your weekly report on all things AI and

language models. Read by over 10,000 others at places like at Google, Tesla, Microsoft, a16z, and more.

11. Welcome to AgentGPT

AgentGPT allows you to configure and deploy Autonomous AI agents. Name your custom AI and have it embarked on any goal imaginable. It will attempt to reach the goal by thinking of tasks to do, executing them, and learning from the results.

12. 192 prompts to 10x your productivity at work

Boost your workplace efficiency with these powerful prompts.

13. Copy.ai

Generate High-Converting Marketing Copy In Seconds With CopyAI. Start Your Free Trial Now! Create Blog Content, Social Media Content, Website Copy, Sales Copy, Ad Copy...

14. 1000 + Midjourney Prompts

Dive deeper into the world of prompts with this extensive collection.

15. MidJourney Prompt Helper

Another insightful tool to further assist in refining your prompt-crafting skills.

16. ChatGPT Cheat Sheet

17. ChatGPT Advantage 250 Prompts Optimized for GPT-4

# 18.  498 Business Prompts

## Need Assistance? Contact Us!

If you require any assistance or have questions, please don't hesitate to reach out to our support team at team@lorean.one for prompt assistance and resolution. We're here to ensure your experience is as enjoyable and enriching as possible. Thank you for choosing our book, and we look forward to being of service!

team@lorean.one

37

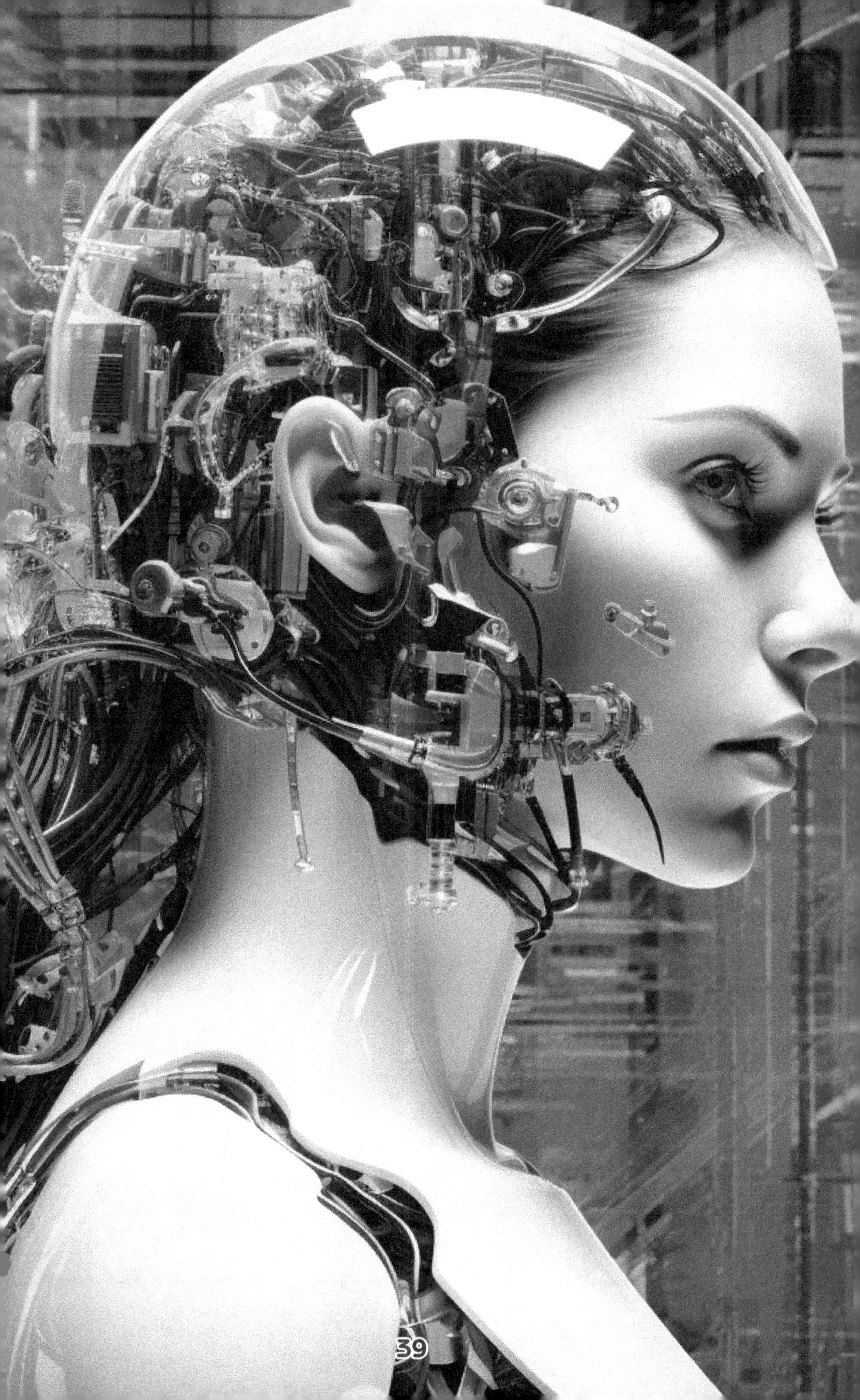

0.0

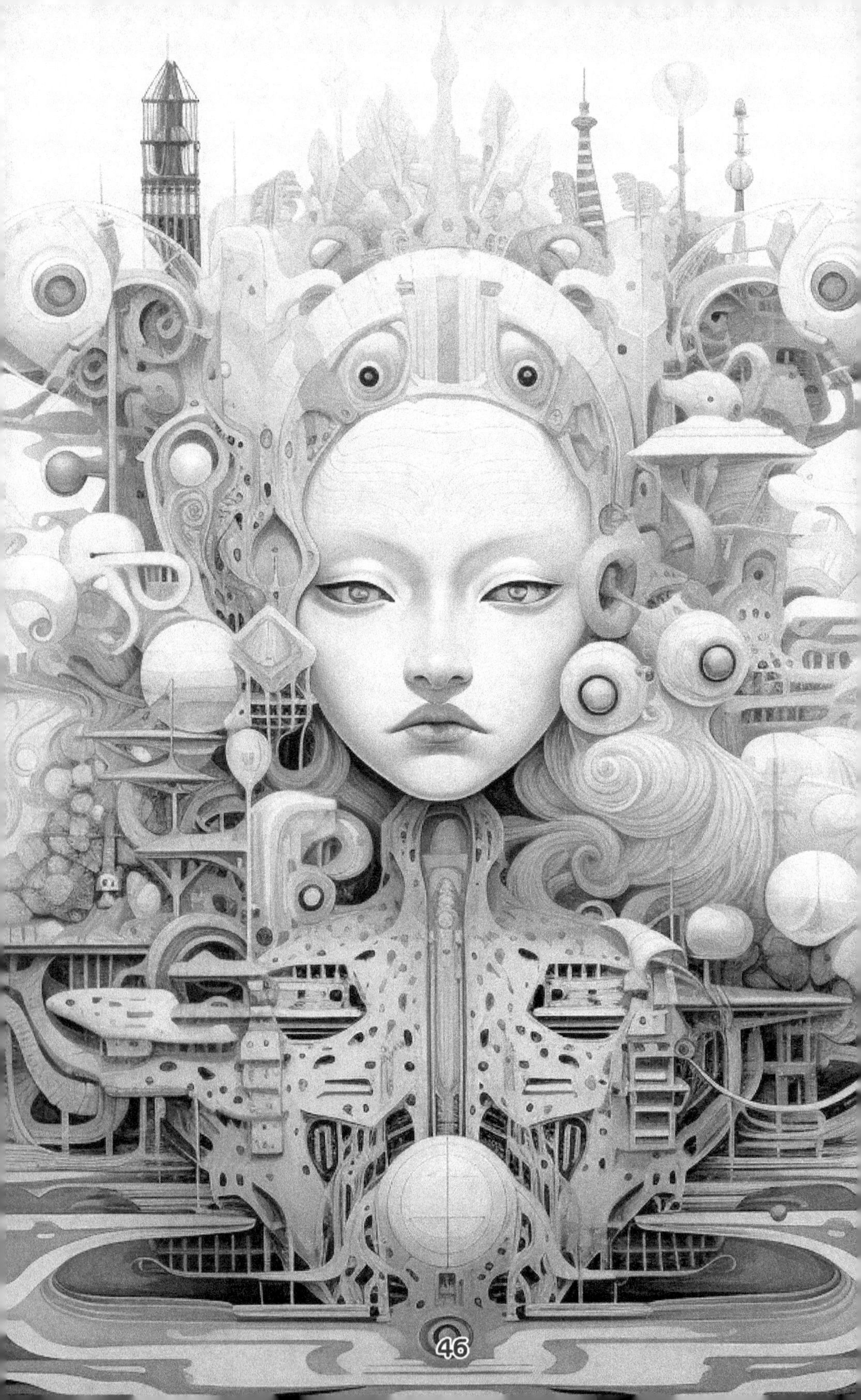

# DIGIDOG

"Unleash Your Curiosity: Discovering the World
A DigiDog Series of Books in Honour of Chico, Our Beloved
Pomeranian"

Welcome to a new series of books, crafted in memory of our dear pet Pomeranian called Chico. For over 15 years, he continued to delight us with his never-ending curiosity, constantly exploring and investigating everything, everywhere.

It is in honour of his spirit of exploration that we present this exciting collection of books that we hope will quench your thirst for knowledge and spark your imagination.

In the series, you will encounter fascinating people with unique life stories, intriguing subjects and the mysteries of the world. Every book provides a number of carefully researched and thoughtfully curated facts that are designed to surprise, enlighten and entertain you.

From the depths of the ocean to the heights of the sky and beyond, our books will transport you to new worlds and reveal the wonders that lie within them. Join us on this adventure and let Chico's legacy inspire you to never stop exploring and learning.

The DigiDog series includes books for both children and adults.
DigiDog is a trade name for Lorean Publishing

# END